BUILD YOUR BRAND TRIBE

THE BUSINESS OF BELONGING
AND RECURRING REVENUE

JASON CJ

.

Published by

SYL+JAS Pte Ltd

Published in Singapore.

BUILD YOUR

BRAND TRIBE

The business of belonging

and recurring revenue

Books also in this Brand Communications series:

bit.ly/sylnjas-brand-comms-series

Mastering Brand Communications

bit.ly/Mastering-brand-comms

ISBN-13 : 979-8568447115

Paperback Price: US$23.90 (ordered

through Amazon)

Ebook Price: US$35.85 (ordered through

publisher SYL+JAS)

F*#@king Audacious Marketing

bit.ly/Fking-audacious-marketing

ISBN-13: 979-8568088578

Paperback Price: US$21.00 (ordered

through Amazon)

Ebook Price: US$31.50 (ordered through

publisher SYL+JAS)

Cultify Your Brand

https://bit.ly/cultify-your-brand

ISBN-13: 979-8571614375
Paperback Price: US$27.90 (ordered through Amazon)
Ebook Price: US$41.85 (ordered through publisher SYL+JAS)

CONTENTS

Introduction

Introduction

From the mid-2000s, relationship marketing became a main influencing marketing paradigm, and the conceptualisation and emphasis on marketing-related relationships has since grown exponentially.

Brand relationships usually take on a few forms and go through ups and downs; comparable to our human relationships. It is interesting how research that has come out on branding and brand intimacy has made comparisons of consumer-brand relationships with analogies that range from things like "acquaintances", "forced marriages", "enslavement", "buddies"., amongst others.

And the fact that we can all connect with these terms and agree with them, is simply the fact that brands themselves have a personality, an identity, if you would. Researchers including Aaker, Batra, Brakus wrote about attachments, love and engagement with brands, cementing the fact that it is all about the relationships that we form with the brands that we are surrounded with.

Grasping the real and present need in committing customers to a long-term relationship, brands have engaged in different forms of tie-ups with customers and have learnt to make adjustments along the way… especially when the relationship evolves too quickly and becomes in a way… awkward. Pretty much like how someone else in school tries to make a move on you too fast, too soon.

14

On the same note, it is also not an easy task to maintain an intimacy that lasts long, especially in a fickle culture that thrives on moving on from one thing to another… with no real commitment. This is where the discussion of creating communities within brands started to flourish. And it is still flourishing today as this book is written.

Brands that build communities will be able to capitalise on reinforcing their customer relationships, and this setup becomes a tool for growing the intimacy and keeping the customer relationship "warm". As with all other relationships, warm is always good.

Brand communities are powerful in that they became a ground for immersing customers in the brand DNA and identity, and are also where the story and history of the brand become perpetuated and in a sense, "indoctrinated".

Through these communities, customers discuss products and services, and also brand extensions, where available. They share their mutual affections and emotions towards different parts of the brand – including the founder or key persons helming the brand. Such connections not just reinforce beliefs, they also create extended relationships that draw in non-committed customers.

Now, because the relationship element is active and present, brands need to realise that in something that is close-knit and intimate, the key to maintaining the relationship is the same as any other intimacy found in human-to-human relationships – and that is STABILITY. To create that level of stability that results in continuity, brands need to understand the process of building relationships before they segue into building communities or tribes, for that matter.

BRAND TRIBE

BRAND TRIBE

In recent times, the zeitgeist seems to suggest a return to times past, and even as far as ancestral roots. This can be manifested even in fashion - the return of certain forms of dressing - the ones that we moved out of a decade ago is now probably being rehashed and coming back in full force in the forefront.

The term "tribe" speaks of a village, nearly pre-historic in its form and at times, ethnocentric. It speaks of shared, heterogeneous sense of values and even emotions.

Tribes in the days of old

According to Britannica, in its anthropological form, a tribe is a social organisation based on smaller bands defined by common descent, language, culture and ideology.

Members belonging to the same tribe jointly endeavour to establish value systems, rules, hierarchies, religion, and common activities pertaining to trade, construction, social order, and even warfare. As they aggregate with other tribes, these clusters eventually grow or subsume more and more until they form larger clusters that include villages, cities, and even nations. When discussing tribalism, there is a need to also dig deep into understanding the concepts of lifestyle, group acceptance and the level of social visibility accrued by individuals within that group.

Another interesting term that has come up in recent years is that of a brand community. The research from Goulding and his team (2013) suggests that this is not a point of semantics/wordplay and that there is indeed a difference between a tribe and community - especially as it pertains to brands.

They posit that firstly, tribes are not a dominant force in the lives of the consumers. Secondly, tribes are more playful than they are concerned with devotion. Lastly, they are transient and passing phases rather than entrepreneurial and are permanent.

This is an indication also that for the most part, when brands talk about generating or creation a sense of belonging, they are really referring to brand tribes, rather than communities per se. This is because of the rate of brand evolution; changes are now happening so rapidly that to transfix a form of permanence in the customer-brand relationship would be akin to assuming a level of faith that is too big for one to hold onto, in and of itself.

Why would customers want to belong to your brand tribe?

Maslow's hierarchy of needs provides a simple explanation behind this innate human nature behind the seeking of self-fulfilment and expression, in addition to having a space of shared experiences.

Hence, when customers talk about the value that a brand brings to them, brand communicators will need to take a deep dive with them to uncover what they really cherish. Because often times than not, the answer to this deep sense of attachment lies in something more emotional rather than utilitarian or hedonic. When this emotional state shifts from deep into extreme, this is when the tribe becomes cult (see our book on "Cultify Your Brand"); and of course, with it, the appropriate challenges that arise.

KEEPING THE LOYAL LOYAL

Many brand communicators miss the point when they define and measure brand loyalty purely in economic-transactional terms. When a particular metric is being fixated at to a point that a customer is merely viewed as a repurchasing statistic to be observed via a data analytics tool, then the cold, calculated nature of the bottom-line machinery will soon trickle into the brand DNA and soon drown out proper brand common-sense.

Brand loyalty finds its psychological roots in belonging. With a myriad of choices pertaining to just about any product or service, customers vote very quickly with their wallets.

On the same note, while there are many reasons why brand defection or fleeting loyalty is becoming increasingly common, there are also studies that reveal members belonging to a certain brand tribe who "experience dissonance" when they partake of other brands.

In the recent decade, influencer marketing and brand communications has come to fore.

This term "influencer" is a symbol of popularity, status, and a boasting of a large following. They are typically content creators themselves who take the time to share their likes, dislikes, tastes and information pertaining to any subject area ranging from fashion and beauty to other everyday things like the car they drive or the food they eat. And course, they are able to capitalise on doing so.

Interestingly, as part of this discussion on tribes, influencers themselves are akin to tribal leaders – they hold sway over their tribal members through interactions, and hence the effect of their marketing efforts, especially in word of mouth, is amplified by many times over.

Brand communicators will do well to ensure that these influencers are treated well given the force multipliers that they hold on their cards. Win one over and the tribe is multiplied – exponentially. A caveat though that this is a double edged sword that cuts both ways.

Advantages of brand tribes

Research has shown that a sense of belonging to a brand increases brand engagement and loyalty. Brand tribes inspire unsolicited participation from tribal members in opposing competing brands.

Brand tribal members buy consistently from a brand over an extended period of time. Brand tribes define and defend their sense of belonging fiercely. The devotion and emotional connection sustain the collective unit. Members of a brand tribe also feel a sense of moral obligation to each other and the brand. This perpetuates brand identification and belonging.

BRAND ENGAGEMENT

BRAND ENGAGEMENT

Brand engagement is still in its growing phase, perhaps due to the fact that the platforms of engagement are ever-evolving.

Brand communicators need to take a closer and practical look at how brand experience and engagement can be designed to influence the emotional and behavioural responses of customers.

Tapping on tribal tendencies

In a way, we are suggesting some form of a return to one's "animal spirit" roots, albeit a really fundamental model that brand communicators can use to build a tribe.

To this end, we ask a fundamental question - What elements evoke a sense of tribalism that makes a tribe, a tribe?

From a macro brand perspective, our Bureau taps on the model espoused by Taute and Sierra (2014) with 4 elements posited –

Communality | Glue | Unity | Guard

as a framework to guide the impact in what brand communicators can do whilst building tribes on their own. We overlay this model with practical steps forward so that brand communicators like yourself can implement them at both a strategic and granular level.

Communality - what behaviours are expected of them to co-exist harmoniously?

Glue - what are the elements that attract and bind your customers together?

Unity - what elements must be present within the social order to create a continued sense of belonging?

Guard - at what level are your customers at in defending the brand?

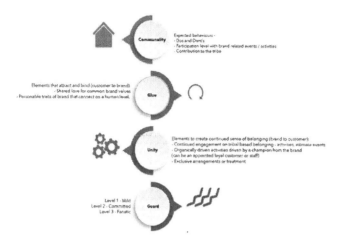

Communality

Expected behaviours -
- Dos and Dont's
- Participation level with brand related events / activities
- Contribution to the tribe

Elements that attract and bind (customer to brand)
- Shared love for common brand values
- Personable traits of brand that connect on a human level.

Glue

Elements to create continued sense of belonging (brand to customer)
- Continued engagement on tribal based belonging - activities, intimate events
- Organically driven activities driven by a champion from the brand (can be an appointed loyal customer or staff)
- Exclusive arrangements or treatment

Unity

Level 1 - Mild
Level 2 - Committed
Level 3 - Fanatic

Guard

40

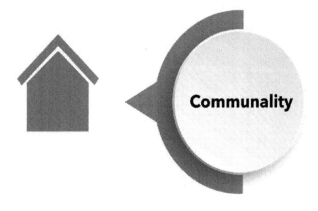

Communality

COMMUNALITY

As businesses and their product/service models will differ, communality is likely to take a different form for each brand.

However, the principles behind communality remain the same. This includes setting the do's and don'ts of tribe members that becomes the default behavioural tone. In the movie Fight Club, albeit a fictitious storyline, underscores the importance of rules - Rule #1 - You do not talk about Fight Club.
This sets the stage for secrecy and an adherence from all members, barring which will result in ostracism or even getting booted from the club.

How would you want the brand tribe members to behave? Is this brand tribe one that is Harley-Davidson-like in nature or Christian Dior-like in nature? Do members need to be a part of a pedigree - and do their behaviours exemplify that class or pedigree?

Participation - this takes place in a variety of ways, including fees / minimum annual purchases, attendance at events. As a brand communicator, there is a need to balance the

44

sensitivities, gauging responses from tribe members and making adjustments. Pilot something before scaling. Test the water to avoid over-committing to a position.

Contribution to tribe - level of availability - / volunteerism. The mutual feeling of belonging to a brand needs to move beyond mere talk. Actions always speak louder than words. Ascertain commitment through participation and contribution. Set up programmes that allow members to take others through an initiation. This could be through, for example, testimonials and membership profile features, etc. Set-up a feedback loop system and glean the potentials for a tribe/engaged-tier of membership.

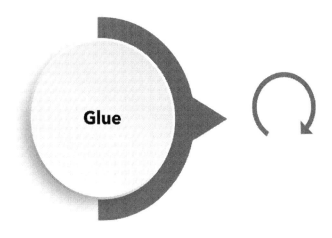

GLUE

When Hedi Slimane took over the Saint Laurent brand, he took the liberty in removing the Yves from the brand name. On one hand, it was viewed as a sacrilegious act. On the other, it played deep into the psyche of his customer profiled who loved the brand value that he, as a brand cult leader, espoused - rebellion.

To this day, at the point of this writing, which is about two years after he left Saint Laurent (and is currently at Celine), the Saint Laurent brand still has a tribe following - on Instagram. They continue to post Hedi-era clothing.

This is what we call a bottom-up initiative - where customers initiate brand-related engagements.

Some may commence organically without an external driving force. Others may require a catalyst or a kick-start to nudge a group to take off in that direction. However, at the end of it all, that engagement needs to be customer-owned rather than brand owned. Without organic momentum, the effort is likely to not gain further traction beyond the initial nudge.

Love and Social Dollars

The concept of brand love is not recent. Brand love refers to the overall sentimental inclination or fondness of customers for a brand. Love in and of itself, is timeless – a human-felt action that came about since the beginning.

While brand tribes are essential in helping customers relate meaningful with the brand, customers will need to 'feel' and develop a deep sense of emotion, love and passion for the brand. It is in this context that brand love is discussed and noted to be the reinforcing link that influences tribes to initiate advocacy or show loyalty towards the brand.

Brand love can be measured in three dimensions – intimacy, passion and commitment, and while we will not be discussing the building of these dimensions within the book, it behooves us to note their importance in building brand love.

In a study entitled "Social Dollars" by Manchanda, Packard and Pattabhiramaiah (2015), the research team investigated the economic returns to a brand from customers that are specifically attributed to the brand's online community.

They concluded with that "social dollars" account for about 20% of the spending of customers after they joined the community. Contrary to popular belief, the researchers uncovered that it is not so much a customer's increased exposure to brand or product information that results in high spending on the brand.

To achieve superlative returns, the brand has to enable or catalyse the "social engagement among consumers over their shared brand or product interests". This includes the creation of "friend" ties and "posting" to one another.

As a brand communicator, one of the things you will need to decide would be the brand values or product features perhaps that attract controversy amongst tribe or potential tribe members.

Then, catalyse or create the impetus for that value or element to be reinforced as a brand narrative. Use data analytics of feedback mechanisms to sieve out members who you can engage to create the needed brand momentum for tribalism to take place.

You will also need to endeavour, as far as possible, to design the features of the tribe so as to be able to observe customer behaviour. This would be a better position to control and determine tribe quality (i.e. your tribe membership quantity is likely to be smaller) than to cede control and insight of your brand's online social activities to a social platform.

Co-creation as glue

Beyond the first and subsequent purchases of customers, many brands struggle to engage them, leaving most conversations to either an organically driven brand effort by loyal customers that is taken outside the scope of control of the brand communicator, or one that is barely alive.

One of the key paradigm shifts within marketing and branding is that of segueing from fleshing out the unique selling propositions of a product or service to getting the customer on board with the brand through various means, and forge intimate, meaningful relationships that are sustainable.

It is on this front that we understand how we should enhance customer consumption experiences, and how this in turn affects customer engagement.

These experiences create a customer-brand emotional bond that results a snowball marketing and sales effect, including repeat purchases, cross-buying, buying more in quantity and even quality (price), and even customer referrals. In other words, the experience attracts people to become part of the brand tribe.

Part of this paradigm shift has led to co-creation, collaboration, and greater personalisation for the customer. This forms a play into the zeitgeist. Brand communicators will need to take stock of current engagement fronts and identify customer segments that respond well to these shifts.

Some ways to go about doing this include:
1. **Exclusivity** - creating a space that members or higher tiers of members can access for collaboration or unlock spaces for co-creation. This generates belonging and plays into the current culture.

2. **Rewards** – There is a marketing momentum that was amplified by games that include Pokemon and similar genres that require participation that result in unlocking of tiers and points. Brand communicators will need to a leaf out of this reward system that keeps participants engaged. This also allows for measurement and monitoring of results.

3. **Collaboration** – There is a rapid shift from mass customisation to mass personalisation.

   Smaller retail outfits like Bynd Artisan understands this concept and capitalises on it to compete with established international luxury brands.

To create the feel of personalisation, the brand has brought their workspace of personalising the leather products to the fore at the retail storefront, where customers can decide on names to put on their leather products – from diaries to wallets and bags.

As customers watch the artisans personalising their purchase for them, it gives them the sense of ownership and participation in the creation of a product that is solely theirs. Other brands that are in the same space are opening up possibilities for personalisation by providing the option of sewing on patches that customers pick out.

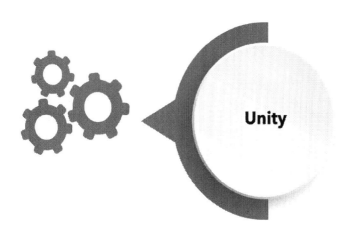

Unity

UNITY

This plays a complementary note to the **Glue** and concerns itself with the brand initiating engagements to nudge a sense of closeness with customers.

Most, if not, all luxury car brands engage at some level of "unifying". activities. For example, Ferrari has an owners' club. An appointed brand champion drives the engagement amongst members.

As a brand communicator, one of the things you will need to decide would be the level of exclusivity or belonging.

This may not necessarily be a financial metric (i.e. amount spent to belong or enjoy privileges). It could be in conjunction with the level of participation (i.e. events attended and average amounts spent, or even amount of tagging done on the brand on their personal social accounts).

Brand communicators will also need to spend a good amount of time in shaping how customers identify themselves with the brand, as this single act of identification will account for a large traction on social media.

Customers that identify with the brand and are connected through social media, will be instant ambassadors in sharing and even checking in on what others think of the brand. With a strong sense of identification forged, such loyal customers belonging to your brand tribe are likely to present and be the voice of the brand in spaces where it is more appropriate for customers to articulate their views rather than for the brand to say something about itself or the values it upholds.

It is critical to note, however, that this form of engagement is likely to expend a lot more resources than if something were to be organic, as with the **Glue** element. Spend energy tightening the relationship to avoid having to spend too much effort with trying to "unify".

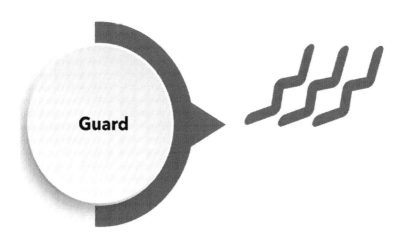

GUARD

Research confirms that strongly connected consumers (towards a brand) do not react negatively to bad press about that brand. Those who are not strongly connected are easily swayed in their opinions. The reason this is so is because a loyal customer's identity is associated to the brand such that the brand forms a part of the consumer's self-image.

For simplicity sake from a brand communications' perspective, we categorise 3

possible levels of brand defence that a brand can accrue from a customer - mild, committed, fanatic.

Typically, less than 1% fall into fanatic. More than 80% are mild or none. And the remaining are fall into the committed category.

What the brand communicator needs to do is to focus most resources in building the **Guard** element on the committed. Not the mild or the fanatic, based on the Pareto's principle (80/20 rule).

Empower and educate through programmes. Ensure that your newsletters or social media touchpoints reinforce areas that you want them to perpetuate through their networks. Through these platforms, you will need to present positive information on the brand continuously to tribe members. This helps to mitigate or minimise negative impact especially during the crisis of the brand.

And of course, reward the reinforcement of their beliefs in the brand - a gift every now and then might just help.

Groom non-customers to be part of the tribe

On a related note, brand communicators seeking to build engagement and commitment can also opt to engage with non-customer segments, even if they are merely at the preliminary stages of association with the brand.

This can be done by tailoring communications strategies to instil within yet to be committed customers a sense of "mental ownership" (Kumar and Nayak, 2019) in the absence of proper ownership of any of the brand's products/services.

This can also be achieved by fleshing out within key brand messages the core values that resonate strongly with potential brand customers.

When done consistently and coherently over a period of time, deeper association with the brand leading towards subsequent conversion to a paying customer who might also become part of the brand tribe, is highly likely.

FORGING INTERNAL TRIBES

FORGING INTERNAL TRIBES

Most discussions about tribes are external facing in nature. Yet this disposition fails to take into account a whole-of-brand approach.

It is on this note that we look inwards and examine brand communications to employees and posit the notion of tribe creation amongst employees so as to buttress the brand from the inside.

Different studies into internal branding recognised the benefits of turning employees into "brand champions". Others examined the roles and expected behaviour of employees in supporting the brand (including Sally Raouf Ragheb Garas et al. (2018), Punjaisri and Wilson (2011), and King (2010)).

The level of coordination between the human capital and the marketing outfits within the brand thus becomes key in creating positive outcomes especially in the area of employees identifying with and being committed to being part of the brand.

As brands have their unique personality and that personality is manifested in their employees and customers who identify and associate with them (whether consciously or subconsciously), then it behooves brands to have a clear branding strategy that aligns both internal and external brand communications.

Particularly with regards to employees, there has to be a tightly-knit, coordinated effort to ensure that the corporate brand is internalised and that it enhances the employee's belonging.

How this may play out could perhaps come in the form of the relooking the criteria in evaluating employees and their orientation/alignment towards the brand. Internal market surveys can be done with employees in order to measure their brand attitudes and behaviour, and also how they perceive the brand.

Managers and directors should be singled out to take on a brand champion role – and this role should be used strategically to drive alignment between internal and external brand communications.

A working level group could perhaps be formed and comprise brand champions from the operational level as well as those dealing with human capital policies and directions. Periodic reviews will need to be conducted to ensure that the alignment is consistent across time periods as incongruent and conflicting messages will likely create dissonance amongst employees and negatively impact internal branding.

BRAND

AUTHENTICITY

BRAND AUTHENTICITY

What is more important than quality? Is there anything else that is more important than quality within a brand? Well, according to research, yes.

And authenticity takes the top spot (Gilmore and Pine, 2007). In fact, the sole contributing factor of authenticity accounts for a number of critical factors to brand success, including customer trust for the brand, brand attachment, greater word-of-mouth marketing from customers, and also the premium price that customers are willing to pay over the average product in that same category.

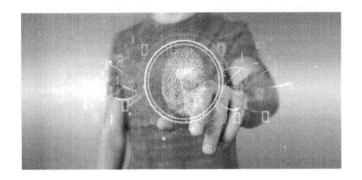

The interesting part behind this discussion is that brand authenticity is not an objective marker. The research clearly shows that even between authenticity and "fake-ness" of a brand is a subjective feature (Grazian 2003), and this perception taken entirely from cues in the market – the very customers themselves!

Oh et al (2019) posit an important framework that brand communicators can deploy to ascertain and manage brand authenticity. It comes with a 4-point model that brand communicators can keep track of in their brand communications plans in managing authenticity:

- **Heritage** – how is the brand maintaining or upholding its traditions? How are customers taking to its brand narrative and history? How else can the brand play on this heritage?

In Singapore, the Song Fa Bak Kut Teh brand is a household name for pork rib soup. They repeat this heritage on their restaurant walls

and consistently treat the "olden days" heritage look through its in-store brand concept and visuals.

- **Quality commitment** – How is the brand investing in quality? And how is this commitment to quality authenticated and communicated?

Following through with the Song Fa Bak Kut Teh brand, the important part of this food outlet is the follow through on quality and commitment. The same taste through the years and level of service. Familiarity that plays into the heritage component is also important.

- **Originality** – how is the brand seen vis-à-vis competitors in its originality? How close behind are other brands in terms of articulating their unique brand position?

The overall brand experience of Song Fa is simple and original, particularly the peppery taste of its soup. While there are competing brands vying for the same customer profile, Song Fa has held onto to being one of the more renowned brands in Singapore. It has at some point in time, also become one of the last food locations to visit for tourists who are flying out of Singapore to another location.

- **Sincerity** – To what extent is your brand following through with being sincere with customers? How is "warm" being defined by your staff members? On the same note, is this feeling of "warmth" being received and reciprocated by customers?

One of the features of the service provided at Song Fa Bak Kut Teh is the fact that the soup bowl of the customer is always topped up to the brim at regular intervals. The nudge to "eat more" is a part of the Chinese culture to be caring to someone else, whether it be paternalistic, maternalistic, or just good neighbourliness.

FROM TRIBE TO RECURRING REVENUE

FROM TRIBE TO RECURRING REVENUE

Part of the brand communicator's role is to bridge initiatives with real dollars to prove value not just for new customers to join the tribe but also stakeholders who are looking closely at these initiatives.

Building tribes by establishing sufficient value to attract members is a tricky thing at the beginning. Gaining those first few members is always the hardest.

Here are some practical tips on overcoming this challenge:

First, go for the low-hanging fruits. Reduce the breadth of the value proposition. Decide what is critical to attract people to want to be a part of the tribe first. Push the rest of the value proposition into the peripheral offer section.

Second, seed highly motivated members into the tribe. This could be influencers who have a huge following base and can inspire others to follow suit. This may require capital to fulfill, but if the effort is well worth it, and the momentum generated can take off, then invest. For those who are seeded to be part of the tribe, some level of involvement is required to entrench them in contributing to brand equity building momentum.

Third, identify and work with like-minded people who can form the base for the tribe, through a partnership of sorts. There needs to be a shared space of values and a present set of raison d'être – clearly defined by the brand communicator.

Leica

Leica is a powerful example of a tribe-built brand. Since the brand's inception in the early quarter of the 1900s, its evolution over the last few decades have led notable photographers like Henri Cartier-Bresson and Robert Capa to swear by it.

The New Yorker ran a 2007 piece glorifying the brand and attempted to elevate it, along with other brand pundits, to that of a cult-like status, but it may be better to at least mention that en route to cult-hood, a tribe is the minimum entry requirement. The copy written was smooth and completely attractive

"What is required is a machine constructed with such skill that it renders every user—from the pro to the banana-fingered fumbler—more skilful as a result. We need it to refine and lubricate, rather than block or coarsen, our means of engagement with the world: we want to look not just at it, however admiringly, but

through it. In that case, we need a

Leica."

*(https://www.newyorker.com/magazine/2007/0
9/24/candid-camera)*

In 2017, its turnover was at more than half a billion Singapore dollars and 1,600 employees. However, with no further technological advancements or new tech related, cutting-edge cameras released, Leica has been able to clock in an entire tribe devoted to the use of its mechanical cameras.

The tribe build-up by the brand has such powerful traction – the famous headshot of Che Guevara was taken on a Leica, and so was the sailor smooching a nurse in Times Square in 1945. Cartier-Bresson's "decisive moments"? Well, you most definitely guessed it.

What steps did Leica take to build its tribe?

Let's examine some of its latest retail in-store concepts as well as currently ongoing efforts to uncover this tribe-building process.

First, it created dedicated Leica-only stores, staffed by people who were knowledgeable in photography. This meant a pure focused play on the brand, creating not only a luxury feel, but also a total control over the store environment without getting diluted attention from other peripherals. The immersion was a welcome move by loyalists and adoring fans.

The internal branding to staff members was also designed to ensure that they bought into the Leica vision.

The stores were also a front to perpetuate the tribe belonging – a gallery space for photography exhibitions as well as studio workshops and other forms of engagement, in addition to the camera sets available for purchase.

This retail branding approach is also employed by Apple, which Leica possibly aspires towards aligning itself in creating a cult brand.

But while Apple launches new technological products every now and then, what does a mechanically driven brand like Leica do? Well, new camera model lines, and other optical products as well, including binoculars, and also its collaboration with smartphone brands like Huawei to extend its reach and co-brand itself.

Above all else, the Leica tribe is cemented with its LHSA – the International Leica Society, created and made open to those who share an interest in the brand and its history. The key officers holding positions in this Society are not Leica staff, which shows how the entire effort has taken an organic format and is self-perpetuating.

What is more amazing is its members' wide-ranging interests from discussions to research and documentation of their Leicas and photographs. And their willingness to pay membership fees of about $1,000 for 3 years.

Paying membership fees grants access to expert advice, the Viewfinder archives, purchase and sale of used cameras and lenses, member discounts of products, amongst others.

Because photography is a unique position in which ownership of a camera simultaneously allows one to co-create, the bonding with the brand is a given. Leica's position in carrying on its legacy of mechanical camera systems automatically cements it in a place of exclusivity.

The authenticity of the brand continues to shine through with its now nearly century long heritage (2025 will mark it centennial). It also continues to play up the brand message to quality commitment through its impeccable manufacturing standards for its line products.

As the community is built into the place of immersed ownership, upselling of products to create the sense of recurring revenue streams from existing customers become a reality.

Now, existing customers account for a majority of purchases – from new camera body kits to lenses. They recommend other enthusiasts to make similar purchases.

Thriving for the future

Has Leica captured its total addressable market? The answer, for now, would be a yes. The brand has longevity and the challenge now lies with getting a new generation of camera enthusiasts interested with what it has to offer with mechanical pieces, like watches.

With the Society, and hence a tribe in place, a recurring revenue model for Leica can take place, albeit one that runs on creating a catch all net for new products to be fed to, whilst feeding existing interests of members.

In setting up similar tribal models, brand communicators will need to realise that the traditional advocacy model that evokes tribalism has to be expanded.

We cannot rely on an old model to function. Newer benefits and offering could include lifestyle benefits, product discounts and access to special events. Be precise in the functional benefit offering.

American Express – Membership has its privileges

Launched in 1958, AMEX, or what American Express is known in short, is seen as a higher status card, as compared to other forms of credit card, regardless of whether it is a VISA, Diner's Club, or Mastercard. With an incessant focus on privileges, AMEX tiers its membership and deliberately segmentises and differentiates its tiers by the willingness to "pay to be recognised".

Behind all this recognition comes the form of tribalism experienced particularly in discussion forums online, that instantly sets the AMEX brand name apart from the others.

In 2015, Marketing Insider Group ran a page
on AMEX's OPEN Forum being the gold
standard of content marketing
(https://marketinginsidergroup.com/content-
marketing/open-forum-gold-standard-content-
marketing/).

How did AMEX achieve this?

This programme provided useful business value to customers and became place for customer acquisition. The AMEX brand communicators saw the opportunity of ensuring that their key customers, in this case, the small businesses, would succeed, and they developed the platform for that to actually take place.

They ran a survey that uncovered about 6 in 10 customers revealing the challenges of using social media, and that only slightly above one in 10 were capitalising on it.

The customers themselves banded together into the tribe through this forum, with a facilitated discussion taking place, and where users can browse, share advice and post questions to help one another out. When LinkedIn came along, the forum embraced it and integrated it as one of its features and social channels, thus enhancing the tribal experience.

From posts that include 6 Tips for Building Community Around Your Brand, AMEX invites businesses to start thinking about how they can engage their own following and deepen that brand relationship. From that perspective, AMEX immediately elevates its status to that of brand thought leader through the platform, instead of merely a card with benefits. This plays into the tribe mentality of receiving and giving aid and help as part of the tribe.

To this end, it scores highly on Originality and Sincerity with its customers and despite the fact that it has the highest percentage charge commission per transaction, businesses keep coming back to them because the sense of belonging to the tribe is one of the contributing factors.

Membership tiers

AMEX's membership pricing strategy is an integral part of its brand communications. By positioning itself as a premium card, it plays into the psyche of "signalling" where people opt for certain brands to convey status. And even within the AMEX customer profile, further tiering takes place. Here are the current tiers based on the annual fee structure:

Everyday Card: $0
Everyday Preferred Card: $95
Gold Card: $250
Business Gold Card: $295
The Platinum Card: $550
Business Platinum Card: $595
The Centurion / Black Card: $10,000 *initiation fee, one off + $5,000 annual (invite only)

The heritage of the AMEX brand of prestige and progress comes about by the way it communicates its tiers to its members.

By deliberately tiering the membership fee, members belonging to the AMEX tribe immediately identify themselves in pecking order – by what you can afford to pay to retain your membership status. The sense of membership progression also allows them to see their progress in life – how and where their achievements have brought them, and what this amounts to in terms of benefits accrued as a member of AMEX. The higher one goes in this tiering system, the greater the level of exclusivity and benefits/privileges thereof.

For members who belong to one of the higher tiers, there might even be a level of collaboration and co-creation that takes place.

A 2019 Singapore-run campaign on The Platinum Card had up and coming business leaders who were invited and featured. Their card annual fee was a non-waivable SG$1,712, and they were called on to be a part of the brand video that had them sharing how indispensable the card has been in their lives.

Some of the Singaporean based organic (non-AMEX owned) online forums have shown that its members and non-members alike make statements that "Guard" the brand and its exclusive nature, displaying tribe-like characteristics, including exchanges like:

Post A: *"The annual fee makes the cardholder not valued. This must be changed all throughout the banking card system of the world"*

Reply from forum member to A: *"Plenty of cardholders feeling valued. Which is why there is still demand for this card. If you think there is no value, don't get it. Simple."*

Post B: The annual fee and benefits makes the cardholder look dumb. One will be stupid enough to spend $1,700 on a card that does not give much benefits.

Reply from forum member to B: " How is it stupid, if you are paying $1.7K for $400 worth of travel and hotel credits each, 1 night stay at St Regis/ W Hotel plus 3d2n stay at Banyan Tree/ Mandarin? I have not even touched on the welcome bonus, Tower Club and Platinum Vibes, Love Dining, Centurion lounges and many other privileges. Sour grapes much?"

(Exchanges found at:

https://forums.hardwarezone.com.sg/credit-cards-line-credit-facilities-243/amex-platinum-charge-card-1716728-135.html)

The interesting exchange brings about much insights as to how tribe members go out to guard their brand.

The brand consistency and quality commitment – signalled by some of its service benefits including the 24/7 call centre, and quick response customer service / concierge, allows AMEX to fly its flag high and keeps the tribe spirit thriving.

CONCLUSION

CONCLUSION

As tastes continue to evolve and technological advancements create obsolescence amongst products and services, what remains steadfast with a sense of longevity are the relationships built over time.

Be it product- or service-oriented brands, the bottom-line remains immutable – in that the very characteristics that elevate a brand to a level of prestige in the eyes of customers to a point where they feel a sense of belonging, can be addressed in order for brands to build their tribes and following.

As a brand communicator seeking to build a tribe, if there is one thing from this book that should stick with you, it would be this:

Think relationship. From there, recall the presence of family and the sense of belonging to a larger body. And the elements that we discussed will flow to the fore - stability, communality, glue, unity, guard, co-creation, rewards, exclusivity, heritage, quality commitment, sincerity, originality.

As much as you cannot force a horse to drink water when you bring it to a watering hole, you will also not be able to force a customer to be a part of your brand tribe. Create the environment to attract. Find what sticks and what doesn't. Adjust and align accordingly.

About the author

Jason CJ is the co-founder of SYL+JAS, a global brand communications house comprising the Atelier, Bureau, Consultancy and Foundry. He has a master's degree in business administration and has a communications degree specialising in advertising and PR. He has been in the communications ambit for nearly two decades with work that spanned international relations to global marketing and brand communications. He has collaborated, advised and consulted clients in brand communications issues across diverse sectors including finance, healthtech, FMCGs, higher education, media start-ups, technology, and not-for-profits.

Made in the USA
Middletown, DE
06 May 2023

30146214R00076